ANIMALS GROWING UP™

HOW FOXES GROW UP

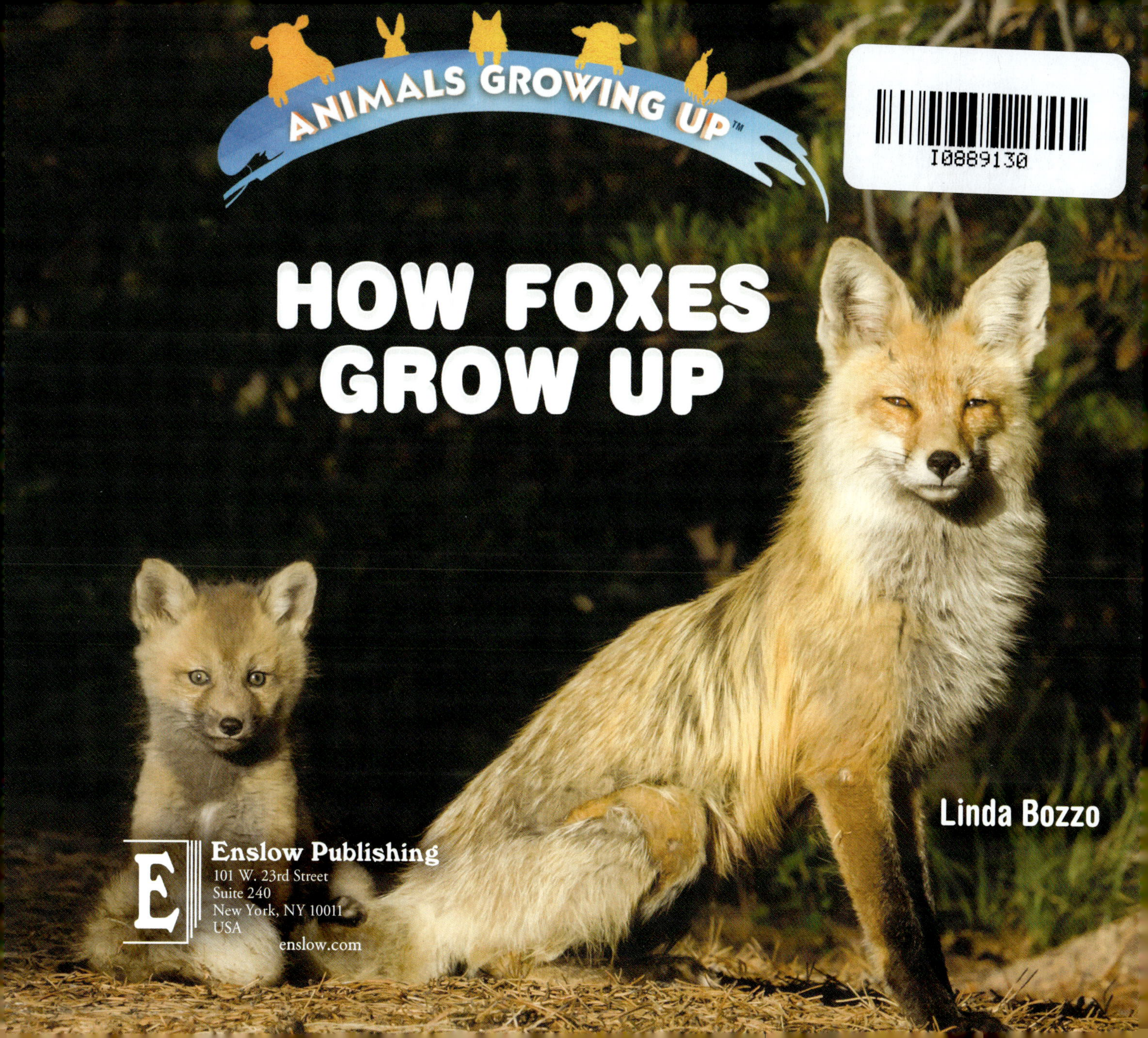

Linda Bozzo

Enslow Publishing
101 W. 23rd Street
Suite 240
New York, NY 10011
USA
enslow.com

WORDS TO KNOW

burrows Tunnels or holes in the ground used by animals.

dens Places where foxes birth and raise their young.

habitats Places in which plants and animals live.

insects Small animals with six legs and a body with three parts that may also have wings.

kits Young foxes.

litter A group of animals born at the same time to one mother.

predators Animals that kill and eat other animals to live.

prey An animal that is killed and eaten by another animal.

romp To run around playfully.

sly Sneaky.

CONTENTS

BABY FOXES

Foxes have long snouts and bushy tails. They are often seen in people's yards. Foxes live in many different **habitats**, or natural places. Baby foxes are sometimes called **kits**.

FAST FACT

Foxes are members of the dog family.

A red fox and her cub enjoy a sunny day.

FOX DENS

Foxes may dig **burrows**, or holes, in the ground. These burrows are called **dens**. Inside the den, kits are born in a nest the mother builds from leaves.

FAST FACT

Foxes only use their dens to give birth and care for their young. They live outdoors the rest of the year.

A fox mother watches her kits leave their den.

LITTERS

Fox kits are born in the spring. They are part of a **litter** of about four to seven kits. Both parents care for the kits.

FAST FACT

The mother fox stays in the den with her kits while the father fox hunts.

This litter of foxes is only one or two days old.

CUTE KITS

At birth, kits are covered with short, dark fur. They cannot see, hear, or walk. They nurse, or drink milk from their mother.

FAST FACT

Kits will become very fast runners. Some foxes can even climb trees!

A mother fox nurses her young kits.

FIRST FOODS

Soon the kits open their eyes. They begin to crawl. But their teeth are still too small to chew meat. Their parents must feed them their first foods.

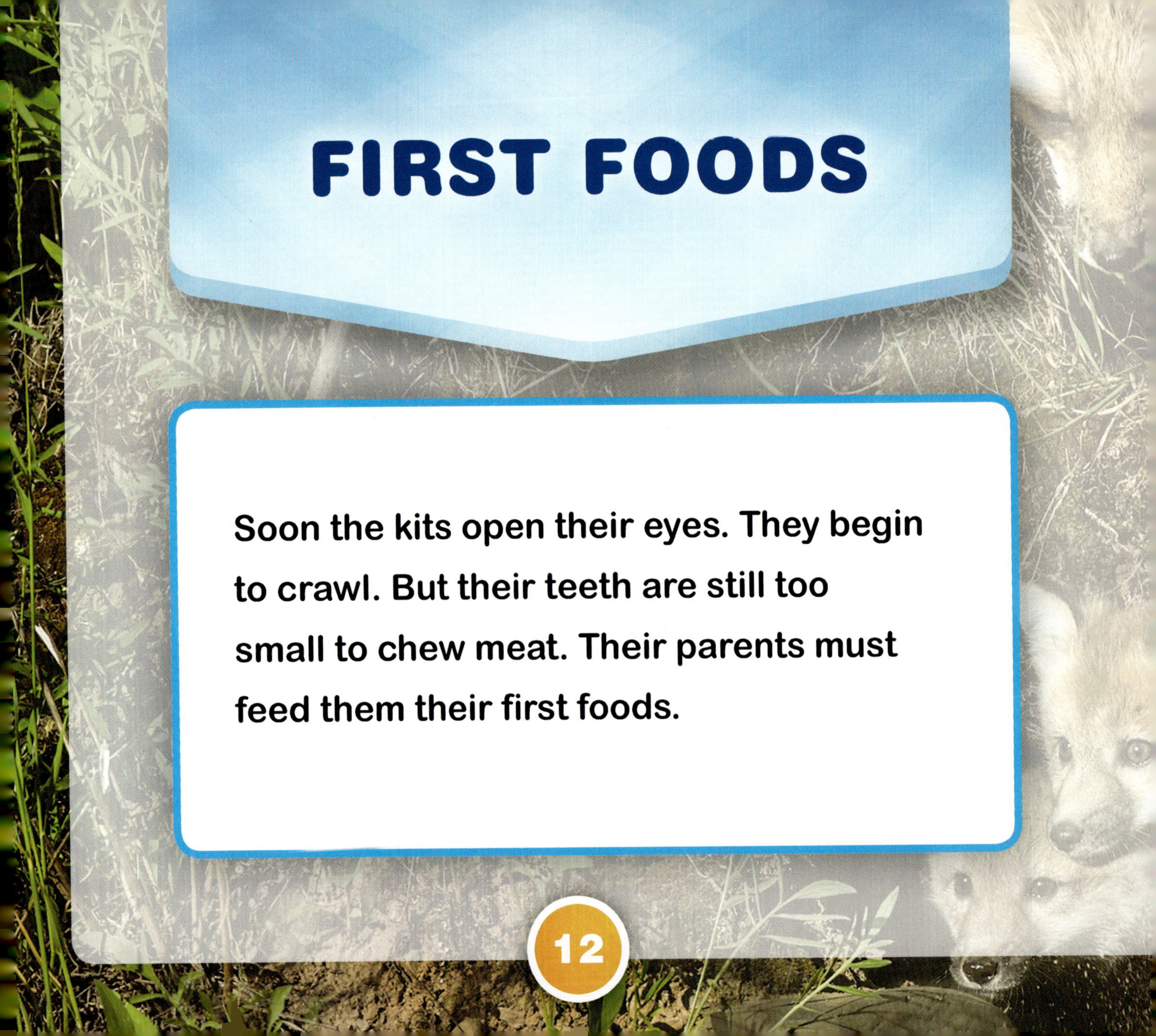

FAST FACT

Adult foxes bring already chewed food up from their stomachs to feed their kits.

A mother fox feeds her kit food from her mouth.

ROMPING AROUND

In just a few weeks, the kits start exploring outside the den. Full of energy, they **romp** for hours. They play with twigs. They chase their littermates!

FAST FACT

Foxes love to play with balls they find in backyards.

Three kits play with each other to learn skills they will need as adults.

FIRST HUNT

As the kits grow older, they roam farther from the den. They are ready for their first hunting trip with their mom and dad.

FAST FACT

Foxes like to sleep during the day and hunt at night.

Fox kits wander out from their den. It's time to help hunt!

SLY FOXES

Kits eat fruits, **insects,** and small animals, such as squirrels, birds, and mice. With their great hearing, these **sly** foxes listen for their **prey** and pounce!

A fox kit runs off with a piece of meat to enjoy.

FAST FACT

Foxes will eat just about anything—even garbage!

KEEPING SAFE

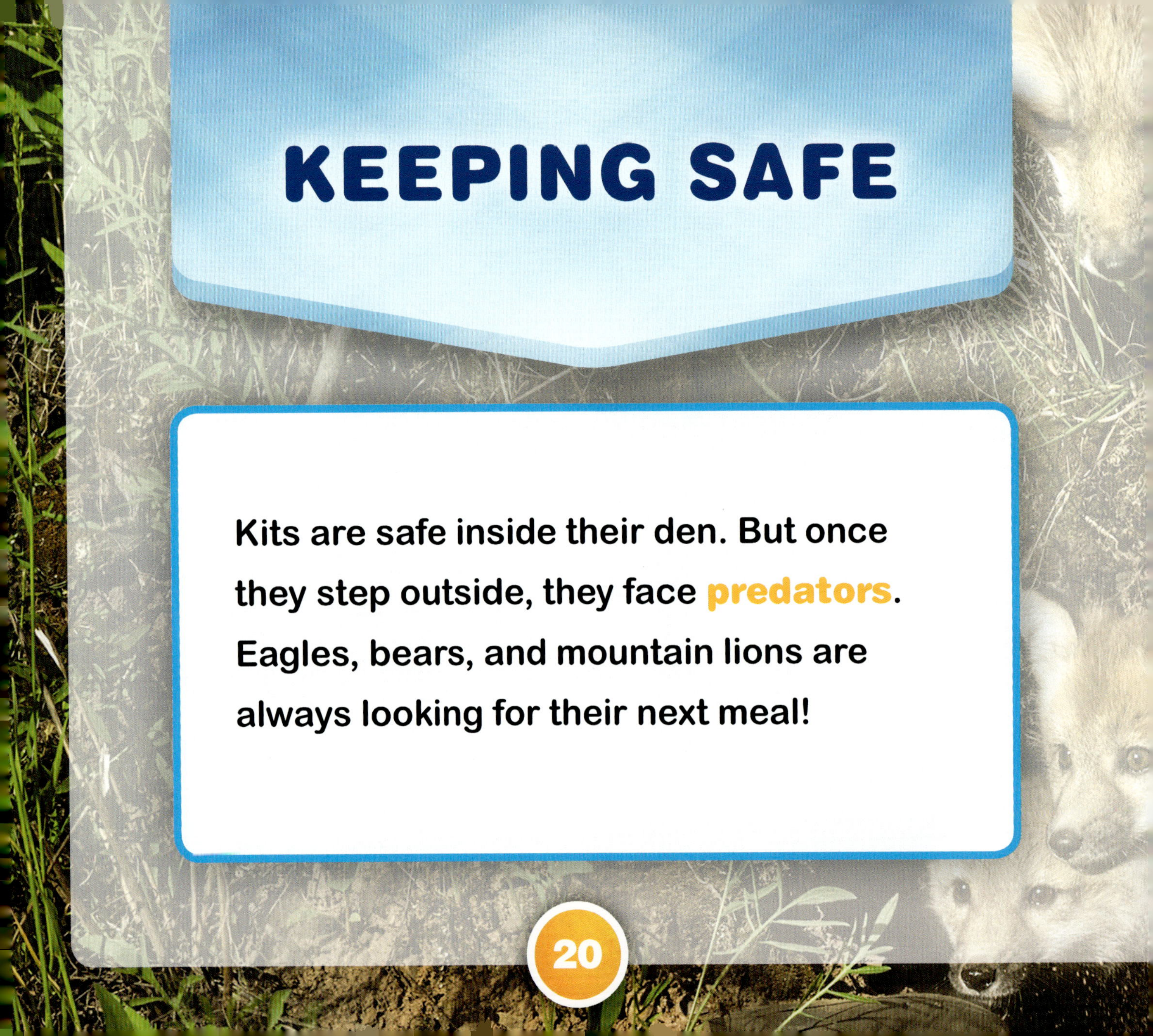

Kits are safe inside their den. But once they step outside, they face **predators**. Eagles, bears, and mountain lions are always looking for their next meal!

FAST FACT

Foxes are afraid of people.

Fox kits out in the open have to watch out for predators.

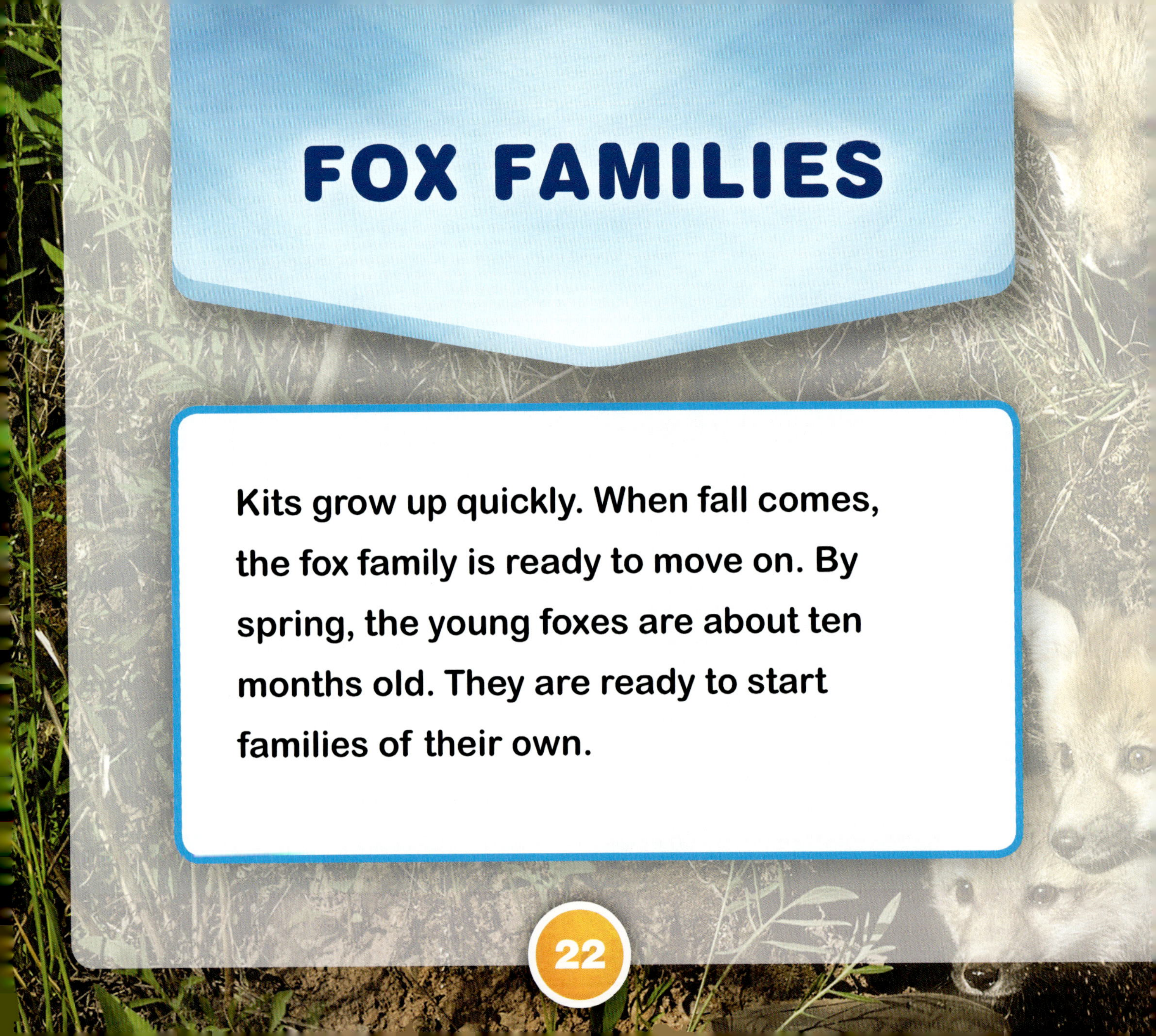

FOX FAMILIES

Kits grow up quickly. When fall comes, the fox family is ready to move on. By spring, the young foxes are about ten months old. They are ready to start families of their own.

This young fox had her own baby. Soon, her kit will start its own life in the wild.

FAST FACT

In the wild, foxes live only about three years!

LEARN MORE

Books

Borgert-Spaniol, Megan. *Baby Foxes*. Minnetonka, MN: Bellwether Media, 2016.
Kalman, Bobbie. *Fox Family Adventures*. New York, NY: Crabtree Publishing Company, 2016.
Riggs, Kate. *Foxes*. Mankato, MN: Creative Education, 2018.

Websites

National Geographic Kids: Fennec Fox
kids.nationalgeographic.com/animals/fennec-fox/
Learn about the world's smallest fox, the fennec fox.

San Diego Zoo: Arctic Fox
kids.sandiegozoo.org/animals/arctic-fox
Read about the Arctic fox and how it survives living in the cold.

INDEX

Published in 2020 by Enslow Publishing, LLC
101 W. 23rd Street, Suite 240, New York, NY 10011

Library of Congress Cataloging-in-Publication Data

Names: Bozzo, Linda, author.
Title: How foxes grow up / Linda Bozzo.
Description: New York : Enslow Publishing, 2020. | Series: Animals growing up | Includes bibliographical references and index. | Audience: K to Grade 3.
Identifiers: LCCN 2019002270| ISBN 9781978512313 (library bound) | ISBN 9781978512290 (paperback) | ISBN 9781978512306 (6 pack)
Subjects: LCSH: Foxes—Development—Juvenile literature. |Foxes—Infancy—Juvenile literature.
Classification: LCC QL737.C22 B626 2020 | DDC 599.77513/92—dc23
LC record available at https://lccn.loc.gov/2019002270

Printed in the United States of America

To Our Readers: We have done our best to make sure all website addresses in this book were active and appropriate when we went to press. However, the author and the publisher have no control over and assume no liability for the material available on those websites or on any websites they may link to. Any comments or suggestions can be sent by email to customerservice@enslow.com.

Photos Credits: Cover, p. 1 Kelp Grizzly Photography/Shutterstock.com; interior pages 4–23 (background), p. 7 Geoffrey Kuchera/Shutterstock.com; p. 5 Menno Schaefer/Shutterstock.com; p. 9 Les Stocker/Oxford Scientific/Getty Images; p. 11 Philippe Henry/Design Pics/Getty Images; p. 13 Maxime Riendeau/500px Prime/Getty Images; p. 15 Ambre Haller/Moment/Getty Images; p. 17 Steve Oehlenschlager/Shutterstock.com; p. 19 taviphoto/Shutterstock.com; p.21 Through Christy's Lens/Shutterstock.com; p. 23 Coulanges/Shutterstock.com; back cover and additional interior pages background graphic 13Imagery/Shutterstock.com.